SHAKE SPEAR SONNETS

SAMIKSHA KUMARI

ISBN 979-888591319-5

Contents

Acknowledgements

This is the first sonnet of Willim Shake Spear.

Sonnet 1

From fairest creatures we desire increase,

That thereby beauty's rose might never die,

But as the riper should by time decease,

His tender heir might bear his memory;

But thou, contracted to thine own bright eyes,

Feed'st thy light's flame with self-substantial fuel,

Making a famine where abundance lies,

Thyself thy foe, to thy sweet self too cruel.

Thou that art now the world's fresh ornament

And only herald to the gaudy spring,

Within thine own bud buriest thy content,

And, tender churl, mak'st waste in niggarding.

Pity the world, or else this glutton be,

To eat the world's due, by the grave and thee.

Sonnet 2

When forty winters shall besiege thy brow

And dig deep trenches in thy beauty's field,

Thy youth's proud livery, so gazed on now,

Will be a tattered weed, of small worth held.

Then being asked where all thy beauty lies—

Where all the treasure of thy lusty days—

To say within thine own deep-sunken eyes

Were an all-eating shame and thriftless praise.

How much more praise deserved thy beauty's use

If thou couldst answer "This fair child of mine

Shall sum my count and make my old excuse",

Proving his beauty by succession thine.

This were to be new made when thou art old,

And see thy blood warm when thou feel'st it cold.

Sonnet 3

Look in thy glass and tell the face thou viewest,
Now is the time that face should form another,
Whose fresh repair if now thou not renewest,
Thou dost beguile the world, unbless some mother.
For where is she so fair whose uneared womb
Disdains the tillage of thy husbandry?
Or who is he so fond will be the tomb
Of his self-love, to stop posterity?
Thou art thy mother's glass, and she in thee
Calls back the lovely April of her prime;
So thou through windows of thine age shalt see,
Despite of wrinkles, this thy golden time.
But if thou live rememb'red not to be,
Die single, and thine image dies with thee.

Sonnet 4

Unthrifty loveliness, why dost thou spend

Upon thyself thy beauty's legacy?

Nature's bequest gives nothing, but doth lend,

And, being frank, she lends to those are free.

Then, beauteous niggard, why dost thou abuse

The bounteous largess given thee to give?

Profitless usurer, why dost thou use

So great a sum of sums yet canst not live?

For having traffic with thyself alone,

Thou of thyself thy sweet self dost deceive.

Then how when nature calls thee to be gone,

What acceptable audit canst thou leave?

Thy unused beauty must be tombed with thee,

Which usèd lives th' executor to be.

Sonnet 5

Those hours that with gentle work did frame

The lovely gaze where every eye doth dwell

Will play the tyrants to the very same

And that unfair which fairly doth excel.

For never-resting time leads summer on

To hideous winter and confounds him there,

Sap checked with frost and lusty leaves quite gone,

Beauty o'er-snowed and bareness everywhere.

Then were not summer's distillation left,

A liquid prisoner pent in walls of glass,

Beauty's effect with beauty were bereft,

Nor it nor no remembrance what it was.

But flowers distilled, though they with winter meet,

Leese but their show; their substance still lives sweet.

Sonnet 6

Then let not winter's ragged hand deface
In thee thy summer, ere thou be distilled.
Make sweet some vial; treasure thou some place
With beauty's treasure, ere it be self-killed.
That use is not forbidden usury
Which happies those that pay the willing loan;
That's for thyself to breed another thee,
Or ten times happier, be it ten for one.
Ten times thyself were happier than thou art,
If ten of thine ten times refigured thee.
Then what could death do if thou shouldst depart,
Leaving thee living in posterity?
Be not self-willed, for thou art much too fair
To be death's conquest and make worms thine heir.

Sonnet 7

Lo, in the Orient when the gracious light

Lifts up his burning head, each under eye

Doth homage to his new-appearing sight,

Serving with looks his sacred majesty;

And having climbed the steep-up heavenly hill,

Resembling strong youth in his middle age,

Yet mortal looks adore his beauty still,

Attending on his golden pilgrimage.

But when from highmost pitch, with weary car,

Like feeble age he reeleth from the day,

The eyes, 'fore duteous, now converted are

From his low tract and look another way.

So thou, thyself out-going in thy noon,

Unlooked on diest unless thou get a son.

Sonnet 8

Music to hear, why hear'st thou music sadly?

Sweets with sweets war not, joy delights in joy.

Why lov'st thou that which thou receiv'st not gladly,

Or else receiv'st with pleasure thine annoy?

If the true concord of well-tuned sounds,

By unions married, do offend thine ear,

They do but sweetly chide thee, who confounds

In singleness the parts that thou shouldst bear.

Mark how one string, sweet husband to another,

Strikes each in each by mutual ordering,

Resembling sire and child and happy mother,

Who all in one, one pleasing note do sing;

Whose speechless song, being many, seeming one,

Sings this to thee: "Thou single wilt prove none."

Sonnet 9

Is it for fear to wet a widow's eye

That thou consum'st thyself in single life?

Ah, if thou issueless shalt hap to die,

The world will wail thee like a makeless wife;

The world will be thy widow and still weep,

That thou no form of thee hast left behind,

When every private widow well may keep,

By children's eyes, her husband's shape in mind.

Look what an unthrift in the world doth spend

Shifts but his place, for still the world enjoys it;

But beauty's waste hath in the world an end,

And kept unused, the user so destroys it.

No love toward others in that bosom sits

That on himself such murd'rous shame commits.

Sonnet 10

For shame deny that thou bear'st love to any,

Who for thyself art so unprovident.

Grant if thou wilt, thou art belov'd of many,

But that thou none lov'st is most evident;

For thou art so possessed with murd'rous hate

That 'gainst thyself thou stick'st not to conspire,

Seeking that beauteous roof to ruinate

Which to repair should be thy chief desire.

O change thy thought, that I may change my mind.

Shall hate be fairer lodged than gentle love?

Be as thy presence is, gracious and kind,

Or to thyself at least kind-hearted prove.

Make thee another self for love of me,

That beauty still may live in thine or thee.

Sonnet 11

As fast as thou shalt wane, so fast thou grow'st
In one of thine, from that which thou departest;
And that fresh blood which youngly thou bestow'st
Thou mayst call thine when thou from youth convertest.
Herein lives wisdom, beauty, and increase;
Without this, folly, age, and cold decay.
If all were minded so, the times should cease,
And threescore year would make the world away.
Let those whom nature hath not made for store,
Harsh, featureless, and rude, barrenly perish.
Look whom she best endowed, she gave the more,
Which bounteous gift thou shouldst in bounty cherish.
She carved thee for her seal, and meant thereby
Thou shouldst print more, not let that copy die.

Sonnet 12

When I do count the clock that tells the time,

And see the brave day sunk in hideous night;

When I behold the violet past prime,

And sable curls all silvered o'er with white;

When lofty trees I see barren of leaves,

Which erst from heat did canopy the herd,

And summer's green all girded up in sheaves

Borne on the bier with white and bristly beard;

Then of thy beauty do I question make,

That thou among the wastes of time must go,

Since sweets and beauties do themselves forsake

And die as fast as they see others grow,

And nothing 'gainst Time's scythe can make defense

Save breed to brave him when he takes thee hence.

Sonnet 13

O that you were yourself! But, love, you are
No longer yours than you yourself here live.
Against this coming end you should prepare,
And your sweet semblance to some other give.
So should that beauty which you hold in lease
Find no determination; then you were
Yourself again after yourself's decease,
When your sweet issue your sweet form should bear.
Who lets so fair a house fall to decay,
Which husbandry in honor might uphold
Against the stormy gusts of winter's day
And barren rage of death's eternal cold?
O, none but unthrifts, dear my love you know,
You had a father; let your son say so.

Sonnet 14

Not from the stars do I my judgment pluck,

And yet methinks I have astronomy,

But not to tell of good or evil luck,

Of plagues, of dearths, or seasons' quality;

Nor can I fortune to brief minutes tell,

Pointing to each his thunder, rain, and wind,

Or say with princes if it shall go well,

By oft predict that I in heaven find;

But from thine eyes my knowledge I derive,

And, constant stars, in them I read such art

As truth and beauty shall together thrive,

If from thyself to store thou wouldst convert;

Or else of thee this I prognosticate:

Thy end is truth's and beauty's doom and date.

Sonnet 15

When I consider every thing that grows
Holds in perfection but a little moment;
That this huge stage presenteth nought but shows
Whereon the stars in secret influence commént;
When I perceive that men as plants increase,
Cheerèd and checked ev'n by the self-same sky,
Vaunt in their youthful sap, at height decrease,
And wear their brave state out of memory;
Then the conceit of this inconstant stay
Sets you, most rich in youth, before my sight,
Where wasteful time debateth with decay,
To change your day of youth to sullied night;
  And all in war with time for love of you,
  As he takes from you, I engraft you new.

Sonnet 16

But wherefore do not you a mightier way

Make war upon this bloody tyrant, time,

And fortify yourself in your decay

With means more blessèd than my barren rhyme?

Now stand you on the top of happy hours,

And many maiden gardens, yet unset,

With virtuous wish would bear your living flowers,

Much liker than your painted counterfeit.

So should the lines of life that life repair

Which this time's pencil or my pupil pen

Neither in inward worth nor outward fair

Can make you live yourself in eyes of men.

To give away yourself keeps yourself still,

And you must live, drawn by your own sweet skill.

Sonnet 17

Who will believe my verse in time to come
If it were filled with your most high deserts?
Though yet heav'n knows it is but as a tomb
Which hides your life and shows not half your parts.
If I could write the beauty of your eyes
And in fresh numbers number all your graces,
The age to come would say, "This poet lies—
Such heavenly touches ne'er touched earthly faces."
So should my papers, yellowed with their age,
Be scorned, like old men of less truth than tongue,
And your true rights be termed a poet's rage
And stretchèd meter of an ántique song;
But were some child of yours alive that time,
You should live twice: in it and in my rhyme.

Sonnet 18

Shall I compare thee to a summer's day?

Thou art more lovely and more temperate.

Rough winds do shake the darling buds of May,

And summer's lease hath all too short a date.

Sometime too hot the eye of heaven shines,

And often is his gold complexion dimmed;

And every fair from fair sometime declines,

By chance or nature's changing course untrimmed.

But thy eternal summer shall not fade,

Nor lose possession of that fair thou ow'st,

Nor shall death brag thou wand'rest in his shade,

When in eternal lines to time thou grow'st.

So long as men can breathe or eyes can see,

So long lives this, and this gives life to thee.

Sonnet 19

Devouring Time, blunt thou the lion's paws,

And make the earth devour her own sweet brood;

Pluck the keen teeth from the fierce tiger's jaws,

And burn the long-lived phoenix in her blood;

Make glad and sorry seasons as thou fleet'st,

And do whate'er thou wilt, swift-footed time,

To the wide world and all her fading sweets;

But I forbid thee one most heinous crime:

O carve not with thy hours my love's fair brow,

Nor draw no lines there with thine ántique pen.

Him in thy course untainted do allow

For beauty's pattern to succeeding men.

Yet do thy worst, old Time; despite thy wrong,

My love shall in my verse ever live young.

Sonnet 20

A woman's face, with nature's own hand painted,

Hast thou, the master-mistress of my passion;

A woman's gentle heart, but not acquainted

With shifting change, as is false women's fashion;

An eye more bright than theirs, less false in rolling,

Gilding the object whereupon it gazeth;

A man in hue, all hues in his controlling,

Which steals men's eyes and women's souls amazeth.

And for a woman wert thou first created,

Till nature as she wrought thee fell a-doting,

And by addition me of thee defeated,

By adding one thing to my purpose nothing.

But since she pricked thee out for women's pleasure,

Mine be thy love, and thy love's use their treasure.

Shake Spear Sonnets

This book was written by William ShakeSpear . There are whole 169 sonnets but in this its 20 only next book will have 20 more and so on.

Printed by Libri Plureos GmbH in Hamburg,
Germany